Read*ux*

Readux Books: Series 5, No 19

Copyright © 1977 Fata Morgana

Translation copyright © 2015 by Ryan Ruby

Originally published as
Petit guide du XVe arrondissement à l'usage des fantômes

All rights reserved

ISBN: 978-3-944801-33-9

Cover by Adeline Meilliez
Design by Susann Stefanizen

Published by Readux Books
Sorauer Str. 16, Berlin, Germany

www.readux.net

A Little Guide
to the Fifteenth Arrondissement
for the Use of Phantoms

Roger Caillois

Translated from the French by Ryan Ruby

For years, I walked, and still walk, once or even several times a week, through the fifteenth arrondissement, more precisely in the neighborhood that today occupies the former village of Grenelle. I witnessed its transformation. I saw the high-rises of the Front de Seine replace its houses, with their pergolas and little gardens, as well as the dilapidated dwellings where, until recently, mostly foreign workers lived. To begin with, I peered through the shop windows: toys, aquaria populated by exotic fish, haberdasheries with their spindly olive-wood sculptures, assortments of fruits, vegetables, mushrooms, dyed cheeses in marzipan. Eavesdropping on the passersby, I tried to guess their places of origin from the words and sounds I caught on my way. Several times I got lost, so I took great pains to familiarize myself with the topography of the area. It can be abnormally misleading. I tried to determine why this was the case, instead of taking pleasure, as I had before, in wandering wherever my fancy took me. I nearly gave myself over to such systematic exploration. Yet it was not this change of objective that inspired me to write a very peculiar kind of guide to this part of the city.

I ended up examining the buildings that, for want of window displays—whose appeal had long since been exhausted—could present less obvious, that is to say less voluntary, objects of interest. In this way, I discovered buildings of a most common appearance, which nonetheless revealed unexpected characteristics upon closer examination, always the same ones, which I was incapable of defining with any precision at the moment, but which I had surely never come across until now. I lingered, I reflected. One day, for fun, I pretended that these residences were intended for the downtrodden people whom their architecture suited so astonishingly well, informing them that they could seek shelter there without fear of error, just as traveling apprentices could tell which lodge in each town would put them up for the night.

Quite willingly, I was led to conclude that they were hideouts reserved for the initiates of some forbidden sect. Everybody knows that crowded places make the best asylum for the hunted. In a desert, it's very difficult for a fugitive to escape his pursuers. He's a marked man. One sees only him.

Someone spots him soon enough. In a big city, by contrast, no one notices him. Without warning, he can hop on a bus, in a taxi, or on the Métro, and that's where the bloodhounds lose the scent. Otherwise, the fugitive can enter a department store by one door and leave again by another. Detective novels abound in such clever tricks, each one as ingenious as the next.

It remained nevertheless to explain the specific strangeness of these safe havens. It occurred to me that, rather than humans, one could shadow the simulacra that resemble them. I remembered a story by Léon-Paul Fargue, entitled *The Drug*, which I've long considered one of the masterpieces of the modern Fantastic.[1] The story concerns floating beings from some unknown Limbo, recognizable by certain mysterious signs. One day, they suddenly congregate in a remote neighborhood; the next, they vanish without warning. They bustle about the city, profiting from the general distraction or indifference, until the moment an informed passerby catches sight of one and decides to chase it to the point of exhaustion. Then things are bound to end badly. They thin out, fade, become transparent, sink into the earth, rise into the air like a balloon a child has accidentally let go of, or otherwise flatten themselves against a porous wall that absorbs them like blotting paper. None of them holds out for long. It's not good for them to have been surprised *in flagrante delicto* "not being men."

The decisive step was soon taken. Some demon tempted me to confirm — just to set my mind at rest — that there really weren't any such things as supernatural beings; and to try in any case to determine instead where people's desire to imagine such things came from. Out of scrupulousness or just for fun, I took to searching for them. Little by little, I began to associate the residences I enjoyed taking stock of in the fifteenth with these untruthful — if not exactly false — creatures. Aided by my own ingenuousness, I gradually came to believe these buildings had been naturally allocated to them. It was the fanciful conjecture of an idle walker. However, I assigned myself this task without realizing that the sole purpose of my wanderings was to catalogue these unusual buildings. I hadn't yet settled on the purpose of my inventory. Would it list the addresses of safehavens or traps? I didn't have any idea. The choice depended, truth be told, on my whims. I put off the decision until later. For the moment, I limited myself to completing as best as I could an inventory that I myself found bizarre, even though I had chosen it myself.

My ordinary route into the fifteenth leads me past the École Militaire. I take pleasure in the majesty of the facade, though it isn't as uniform as it initially appears. It gives the impression of a rigorous symmetry. Each wing seems to be the exact duplicate of the other. But upon closer examination, they aren't mirror images. On the roof of the right wing, four monumental chimneys stand at attention at equal intervals. The left wing has only a single thin one, at the far end, which clashes with the ponderousness of the chimneys on the other side. The difference jumps out at you as soon as you notice it, but the need for symmetry is so deeply ingrained in people that almost no one perceives the quite visible breach; many have even refused to believe me when I pointed it out to them. Time and time again, I have had to stand a skeptic right in front of the building for him to yield to the evidence. There is nothing very surprising about such an anomaly— or the resistance it usually provokes. But having already found myself on the Way of the Strange, it wasn't long before I saw in the dissymmetry of the École Militaire the warning that beyond this frontier, the order of things, or at least architectural customs, had changed. Just so, in the film *Nosferatu*, a semi-solemn title card warns the spectator of the dangers that await the hero: "*And when he had crossed the bridge, the phantoms came to meet him.*"

I had already seen the film in Paris, about a year before I left for Germany (circa 1930) for a student exchange just as that practice was becoming popular. I watched it again in the cinema in a neighboring town. I returned through a pine forest to the little village of Jößnitz where I lived. It was a clear night. As I was about to cross the railway bridge that marked the midway point of my journey, I suddenly saw before my eyes — just as I had seen it on screen not long before — the fateful card. I remember feeling terrified, not without playing my part, I suppose. At any rate, the text on the title card must have made quite an impression on me for it to come back to me now, without warning, after so many years.

After the École Militaire, you cross the Avenue de Suffren and enter the fifteenth arrondissement, whose first building occupies the corner of the Rue du Laos. The house leans sideways and doesn't abut the next one. Forming a pronounced acute angle, it juts out awkwardly, so that, from a certain perspective, it doesn't seem thick enough to give anyone shelter. A number of the residences in the neighborhood I was exploring were constructed on the same incongruous model. A profile just as thin, sometimes crenellated by toothing-stones, rises in the sky without anything leaning against it or fitting into it. The corner is left in limbo, forming a beveled edge so narrow that it must have discouraged architects from constructing the complementary building. The adjacent corner would be excessively obtuse and the room that it delineated would be set too far back on the outward-facing wall. Without a doubt, it was these very buildings that so deeply attracted my attention when I was still incapable of clearly formulating what it was that made them so singular. Now I understand. It seems to me that, from the start, my walking has had no other purpose than to acknowledge their existence.

I don't know what capricious urbanism scattered such inconvenient curiosities throughout the arrondissement. Here and there are examples, all isolated and just as baffling with their razor-thin edges. Remarkably, they begin to appear right after the Avenue de Suffren. None are to be observed before this boundary line, but they become common after the little Square de la Motte-Picquet that follows soon after the Village Suisse. The Rue d'Ouessant begins there. Not far from the spot where, according to the offhanded geography of the area, the Rue de Pondichéry cuts off the Rue du Soudan, there stretches the Dupleix school complex, a one-floor modern construction of bright red brick. Through the huge bay windows, the classrooms are flooded with the warm light of the sun. A tree-lined playground enfolds a sunny spot of greenery. All is cheerful, pleasant. One senses the excitement the children bring to each recess. So it's regrettable that a space devoted to carefree joy is dominated by an immense blank surface, a dismal, peeling wall, punctured on each floor by three, four, or five quadrangular openings which sink back into a uniform dullness, and don't even look like windows. The wall exudes false neglect and insidious hostility.

It was without question just a dilapidated building, marked for imminent destruction. But its presence seemed no less ominous for it. Moreover, the sinister house presented the fateful cutaway, the strange sharp edge that seemed inhabitable only by flat beings, immaterial beings, just as in the story by Fargue.

If you pass Boulevard de Grenelle and follow Rue du Commerce until you reach Avenue Émile-Zola—that grand artery that returns to the Seine right where the superb towers have just finished being constructed—all of a sudden, on the left, the anomaly repeats itself, more complex, and I dare say, more revealing.

On both sides of the building at 152 Avenue Émile-Zola rise two apartment buildings, six and seven stories respectively, also with acute and crenelated edges. In this neighborhood of shops and banal business, they inexplicably appear to trap an infinite space between two scenery flats. Until recently, 152 was occupied by a crimson shop, always shut, whose pompous sign *Halle de l'Economie* stood in marked contrast to its sordid character and modest dimensions. Today it has been replaced by one that reads BIJOUTERIE-HORLOGERIE. Two billboards take the place of a missing top story. Far behind it extends the back of a building that looks out on another street. It seems to round out the scene delimited by the two scenery flats, which, if you can believe it, is in no way empty. Indeed, the entire right half of the wall is covered by a mural, which offers to the gaze of passersby an old-fashioned kitchen with stoves and saucepans. A sturdy housewife lifts her arms to the sky, filled with wonder at the monstrous sack of coal brought to her by a jolly deliveryman who bends under its weight. The mural calls to mind a bygone age, although the colors are still fresh. A little later, I discovered by chance in a shop window on the Rue de Seine a photocopy of the original work: a promotional illustration by Robert Daumier commissioned by Ivry Storage, a firm that undoubtedly no longer exists.[2] Enlarged and painted, numerous copies of the composition were spread over the empty walls of the city and its suburbs.

Paris, I remember, was then decorated by such gigantic, painted advertisements. To the real population that bustled in the streets, they added to the prestige of an everyday empire, an assembly that may have been scattered and disparate, but managed nevertheless to iterate effigies of its demigods. Immense, immobile, occupying the tops of the tallest walls, they observed, beneficently or sardonically, the commotion below. The image of domestic prosperity that suddenly surged before me on the Avenue Émile-Zola recalled to mind a marvelous procession of figures. I had neglected it somewhat, on account of its trivial subject matter, denuded of all mystery; although truly marginal, it belonged no less to the mythology that had fascinated me during my childhood. Issuing spontaneously from my surroundings, I understood it directly, without having to learn about it from grown ups or books. Its secret powers I alone had divined and entertained.

I felt a sudden affection for the person at Ivry Storage who had commissioned the mural. I reproached myself for having looked down on the man. Thanks to him, the universe in which I had lived out the first and decisive years of that second life that accompanies our conscious reveries, was restored to me: a collection of unexplained affinities that guide us without our realizing it, a spell whose origin escapes us and takes us prisoner. Now, after many years, chance had admitted me to the occult universe from which these hidden phantasmagorias had emerged. With delight I was reintroduced to fabulous figures. Again I saw, not without pitying them a little, Napoleon, Louis Phillippe, and Marianne, Symbol of the Republic, whom some malicious sorcerer had stuffed into a washbasin for the greater glory of a laundry detergent. A leaping green demon spat scarlet flames skyward, wildly clasping incomprehensible swarms of white to its chest. He was recovering but I imagined that an intolerable torture had been inflicted upon him. A dazzling black lion showed off a sinuous tail high above his splendidly ferocious, muscular body. But I was more frightened by the two giant, overlapping moons, one pale and laughing, the other somber and in tears, the first beginning to obscure the second (or the other way around, I don't remember anymore), in order to assert the merits of a shoe cream. I worried that an eclipse of the real moon would take place, which I interpreted as a catastrophe, with which I was complicit.

Above all, I had taken a large man dressed in black for an evil genius, a man whose name a half a century has not totally erased from my memory. He was called something like Villiod. The evening cape in which he was wrapped revealed a white waistcoat and tails. Behind a mask just large enough to obscure his true identity shone eyes, which never allowed the slightest detail to escape. This contemporary and doppelgänger of Fantômas held in his two hands an enormous key that crossed his body at a menacing diagonal. As it was so massive, the key's teeth extended high above his concealed face and, at the other end, its ring rested at the level of his knees. This magical weapon made him all-powerful. If I'm not mistaken, the stranger's motto, inscribed on the poster with his name, was "celerity and discretion." I doubt I was familiar with the meaning of the first term, which only made it seem that much more awe-inspiring. Nor was I aware of the invisible empire under the despotic control of this sinister apparition. I suspect I wasn't of the age, at least not yet, to fall under the jurisdiction of his mysterious legislation. However, there would come a time when I would have to fear him still more than the men in white coats whom I had glimpsed in a hospital and who now staffed my nightmares. It was a fear I massaged and measured out as I wished, a fear that converges with pleasure, like in a ghost story. In fact, I soon enough ceased to be in awe of him. One fine day, I even came to identify with him. Still later, the man with the key embodied for me an anonymous and ice-cold intelligence that endeavored to penetrate the enigmas of society and nature. The character in formal dress, solemn and masked, formed a couple with the romantic, naked, riotous, fire-breathing green demon—who also continues to haunt my memory. In the intervening period, I have learned that one advertised a detective agency and the other the effectiveness of medical cotton. In the end, to my great surprise, I discovered they were both the work of the same man, Jean Cappiello, a painter who had devoted part of his exceptional talent to advertising posters.[3]

Today the poster of Villiod is impossible to find. In vain, I asked for it at the Print Room of the National Library, at the Copyright Office, at the Museum of Decorative Arts, at specialty shops. You would think it never even existed. Still, the figure sketch in the monograph Capiello's son-in-law devoted to him: many remember it. Nelly de Vogüé even recalls having seen the detective's silhouette printed on the spines of the telephone directories of the era.[4] No matter: I'm almost as pleased by its abnormal disappearance. It confirms the fantasy-nature of the image.

Surely it wasn't without reason that such images—warning signs, controls, or signals—found themselves distributed here and there on the windowless walls of buildings and on the lustrous tiles of the stations of the Métro. This promotional mythology—whose real function children are more or less unaware of anyway—has disappeared today, replaced by paper posters in reduced formats, which, changing constantly, can't possibly make a lasting impression on memory. They are torn down quickly, worn down by bad weather, one after another. They lack that timeless aspect as well as that inaccessibility that, for an insatiable and still-naïve imagination, confers on ancient frescos a quasi-miraculous character. To be sure, the unreal signs were themselves only advertisements, but at the same time they were possessed of the authority of the legendary, which trumped their commercial purpose. They added their own magic to the urban décor and, at the age when fairytales and experience are still all mixed up, they peopled the long, tedious errands on which children are uselessly forced to accompany their parents with familiar apparitions.

The walls of Paris, it seems to me, have not since seen the equal of Villiod, the man with the key. The universe that began with the housewife and the coal deliveryman ended with him. That's why I found myself profoundly moved when the fragile painting between the two beveled buildings on Avenue Émile-Zola resurrected for me the buried world that first formed my sensibility, a sensibility that sometimes seems to have emerged more directly from it than from my human parents. I insisted on interrupting my tour of the fifteenth arrondissement to pay homage to a vestige of the past that, in my eyes, is more meaningful and more important than historic buildings like Sacré Coeur and the Grand Palais. I write in honor of the imagination I've outgrown. In addition to the reverence I owe Villiod, I am lead to believe that, at this point in my argument, the imagination deserves a place I hope I will not be the only one to acknowledge.

Closing this parenthesis, I take up my itinerary once more and make my way further down the Rue du Commerce, until I reach the butcher's shop at number 78. Again, a simple ground floor, this time with a curved pediment trimmed with sober molding that stands in for a second story. Two blind windows were added at the center, where they were flanked by black, semi-circular marble plaques on which golden letters once boasted of the quality of the meat sold within. Only one of them—which still announces that here one finds the best merchandise at the lowest price—remains. In the place of the other, a hole looks onto a gangrenous wall, which no one has bothered to restore.

I assume that more than one shop in the neighborhood elevates itself with a fake second floor in order to attract a clientele. It's a standard trick. Here, it is nevertheless portentous, because it illustrates in its own way the particular architecture that comprises the object of my study. Not far away, it reaches heights of absurdity that defy expectation. I'll return to it later.

For the moment, follow me into the Rue du Théâtre, which leads to a theater right at Rue de la Croix-Nivert. Although it is unquestionably dingy, it has loges, a parterre, and balconies. It is now a converted cinema that makes use of an unorthodox system of programming. While a different film is screened every day, the weekly schedule is organized according to genre: the settling of scores between Indian braves and pioneers in the American West where violence and kindness are combined; adventures in acrobatic combat, judo, or karate where the poses of classical ballet are reinvented; stranger still, reels of historical or imaginary "colossi" like Samson, Spartacus, Maciste, and Houdini, where historical or fantastical glamor plays a leading role, but at the level of cheap trash, of crudeness; and finally, the Wednesday matinee of erotic films whose title is almost always in the feminine plural: *The Insatiabelles, The Luxuriettes, The Unsatisfemmes, The Depravitines, The Impassionatas*, etc.—a significant collection psychologists ought to study in order to auscultate a little more precisely the tenacious dreams, the atavistic ruminations, of the humbler part of the population of contemporary Paris. Very probably, they express aspirations much more widespread and deep-rooted, in the species and even beyond.

The emergency exits of the former theater at 55 Rue de la Croix-Nivert open onto the ends of a drawn-out horseshoe formed by the Rue Meilhac and the Rue Auguste-Dorchain. Curved and austere, a single facade occupies the full length of the Rue Auguste-Dorchain. It culminates in the most perfect beveling, which I have already mentioned: a sharp edge that bears the vertical inscription BAINS-DOUCHES in capitals made from large nails with nickel-plated, reflective heads. They take up the whole thickness of the terminal rostrum. If you stand at the edge of the sidewalk in front of the Bar du Soleil, a kind of annex to the cinema, only the bevel of the long facade is visible; the illusion of a two-dimensional building absolutely imposes itself on you. No one, except for beings of infinite sliminess, could live in this guise of a house, which only regains consistency as you pass the fine, ship-like bow and the high blind wall, which slowly broadens as it closes the edifice round the back. The buildings, with their changing perspectives, now reach the heights of that demented style they follow. Nothing, absolutely nothing prohibited the construction of orthogonal residences here, like everywhere else in the city. The proof is that the building has remained isolated and overlooks an unused area it would have been easy to build up as much as one wished. What was the reason then? The ill will of stubborn heirs who refused to give up so much as an inch of their strangely cut up inheritance? One would have to reconcile oneself to an explanation of this kind, if the sheer number of examples didn't prohibit it.

If you go back down the Rue Letellier you will reach a Villa of the same name. The private road is only a cul-de-sac, but it's spacious. The different houses that line it are at first sight identical, of a mediocre simplicity. With the exception of those on the ground floor, the windows are devoid of shutters, a rare thing in Paris. They are in rows, each exactly five floors of the same height, which confers a rebarbative monotony on the whole ensemble. One could even believe that a single building surrounded the entire alley, if the last house on the left didn't feature a cornice on which elaborate molding alternates with polychrome tiling beneath the second floor. Above the windows of the fourth floor also runs an unobtrusive line of plain crenellations, which undoubtedly consummates the vague desire for ornamentation initiated by a coquettish owner.

These decorative edgings continue, incidentally, on the house that occupies the end of the cul-de-sac. Not as tall as the others, it has only four stories. The windows are always shut and the parallel wooden slats are perpetually drawn. The ruined door no longer has a lock. The door number was ripped out long ago, or maybe the house never had one. Above the entry, a rusty wall lamp must not long ago have been fitted with an electric bulb. Now, a bundle of wires sticks out of the socket like a cluster of dry brambles. On each side, the window shutters of the ground floor are also always shut.

In the central window of the last floor, the worn-out awning hangs from a cracked wall. The house doesn't exist. The facade is attached—it is real and not painted—to the back of another building. To catch the subterfuge, you would have to look at it from up close. But who would dare?

The trick house corresponds to an altogether very natural, even ingenious artifice. After all, it was best to use the blank surface. The residents were obviously loathe to hand it over to advertisers, but refused, on the other hand, to cover it with vines, discouraged by the cost and effort that would be required for their upkeep. Still, the chosen solution almost definitely calls to mind a trap. The imagination suspects the optical illusion to lead to a less innocent ambush. The door without a lock, the stubbornly mute awnings and shutters don't lead one to presume the house is abandoned, but rather that it is used as a hideout, a den. One wants to lure someone there, someone who, paradoxically, will not be able to enter.

After the beveled houses, the simulated house acquires a kind of dreadful import. Without any thickness or volume, it fools, first of all, the fluid beings that squat in big cities and which a poet's narrative taught me to recognize and to track down.

I don't have, as far as I'm aware, the soul of a persecutor. However, I am delighted to have discovered all by myself such a secret. I feel pride to the point of puerile satisfaction. If the need should arise, I will know to take my quarry to the deceptive facade. It will make him believe that he has before him one of the thin residences where he is accustomed to take refuge. Then he'll be trapped. Like a rat.

I amuse myself with these kinds of vagaries. As a child, I enjoyed imagining, while I strolled along the street, stories about vigilantes, avengers, and outlaws. It is only late in life—when the old mental cinema switches on semi-automatically—that I am struck by the fact that, of all children's playthings, adventure books have proven to be the most durable. I continually escaped the daggers of the agents of the Cardinal and the spies of the Counsel of Ten. At every coach gate I evaded the nooses of Thugs dispatched from the sanctuaries of Benares to strangle me. An evil genius, I climbed in the shadows, relentless and secretive, the echelons of power. The only difference: today I require more evidence, indices, verifications. I am less given to fantasy. I expect a greater consistency from my fabrications. I no longer play, exactly. I play at playing. I entertain myself knowingly. In short, I only practice.

The neighborhood, however, is changing with feverish haste. The old buildings are knocked down by the dozen and are replaced by massive and uniform apartment blocks. Most often made up of prefabricated units, they present, almost necessarily, a severe and mechanistic aspect. It entails a grid plan that makes use of the entirety of the available space, an economic requirement to which precisely this type of construction is intended to respond.

Thus: no more acute angles, no more escheated spaces, ever fewer deceptive facades and blind walls. The four exterior surfaces of these structures are interchangeable and are likewise punctured with identical networks of apertures, themselves quadrangular.

Among these unvarying formations of tall towers and fleeting promenades, the private driveway known as Villa Croix-Nivert offers passersby a visual effect that ostensibly slights the regularity that is otherwise the norm. The road is made up of a dozen of the wide blocks of the general design. It stretches approximately from the theater-cinema where we lingered earlier to the Rue Cambronne. Nothing disturbs the impeccable, blank alignment of the cubical towers with their symmetrical openwork. Nothing: apart from the inexplicable commotion of the exquisite shanties stacked up on top of them like roofs or terraces.

Shacks made of a delicate black polished slate gleam in the sun. They cram their squat masses into a space where only sharp, irregular angles are to be found. Insane obliques divert the gaze. Absurd inclines tip them into the void. Unexpected nooks open up vacant spaces that send shivers down the spine. Crannies gape or close themselves up without warning. Everything seems calculated to produce feelings of absurdity and vertigo. Here and there, dwarfish or gigantic door frames, deliberately irregular. Further on, trapezoids joined at their bases like the blades of a two-headed axe, jagged contours, an architecture of collapse, tumult of mangled and muddled hovels arrested in their fall by the contradictory necessities of their own inertia. Only gnomes, those beings with misshapen bodies and minds, whose image is by no means orderly or reasonable, could conceive of such a topographic hell as a normal or desirable habitat. A harmony alien to humanity—which, to my surprise, I found myself appreciating—emerges nonetheless.

Here and there on the ground, along the pathways that divide up the housing complexes, sturdy cement rims protect shafts that are too tall to see into their depths. The last ones, situated at the end of the alley that borders the Rue de l'Amiral-Roussin, are likewise provided with a cement cover that is proportionate to their size. At least ten centimeters thick, they lean above the opening, as far as one can tell, at an angle of around thirty degrees. They are propped up by eight iron bars, the highest being three or four times as long as the shortest ones. The slanting covers are surrounded by a gutter, undoubtedly for drainage. The openings, more than two meters in diameter, must serve as ventilators for basements and garages. I have difficulty, however, understanding the point of such powerful valves. They seem built to outlast the very buildings they serve. Never have casemates or ramparts been reinforced with airways as ample or well-protected, and one wonders what extraordinary menace required a shield of such solidity, when it was, in principle, only intended to facilitate the entrance of an imperceptible and invigorating vapor. Did someone fear the possible eruption of something immense, supple, creeping perhaps, but also capable of bursting through concrete of normal thickness?

The idea of a malevolent creature, of an unknown nature, that we will have to accommodate or capture, seduce or paralyze when the time comes, soon works its way into the imagination. There it associates with the chaos of inhabitable polyhedrons whose dark mass crowns the whiteness of the functional buildings so unexpectedly. Who are their vicious angles, their aberrant profiles, their obscene volumes intended for anyway? Once it heads down such a slippery slope, the imagination is quick to recognize in these very buildings modern replicas of the unwritable slums that feature so prominently in the chronicles of Lovecraft. They have the same geometry that Lovecraft's architects—those traitors to the human race—are said to have prepared, leaving a space for a lethal crevice, at once infinitesimal and immense. The junction of accursed inclines determines the sole angle by which abominable beings, born of an eternally forsaken universe, could break into our own. A fissure in an expanse of concrete permits communication with the parallel pouches where repugnant fetuses and larvae swarm, with their noxious miasmas or deadly gazes.

I have often wondered why so many readers are fascinated by a writer of contrivances as makeshift and dull as Lovecraft. He contents himself with tirelessly amassing negative adjectives like indescribable or inexpressible, unwritable or unnameable, to emphasize horror. Fear, however, would erupt all the more insidiously from a sober and precise picture, which wouldn't ever require the author to use the adjective *frightening*.

My guess is that the kind of hypnosis that emanates from his best stories stems from the tiny but effective discovery that in dilapidated and dusty houses there are corners so malignant and poisonous, so devious and perverse, that in all probability they couldn't pass for the work of human hands and that it would be more economical, so to speak, to utilize them as gateways to energies so accursed that even to recall them would be dangerous.

Obviously, I do not for a moment imagine that the developers who are currently transforming the former village of Grenelle have been mysteriously bribed by the followers of the carpenters of Arkham, Innsmouth, and Dunwich to lay out gravitational fields, favorable dihedrons, traversable buttonholes and, in a word, every gap that would be necessary for an infiltration by crossbreeds of Lemuria and the abyss.[5] The fact remains that the eccentric and angular superstructures of Villa Croix-Nivert evoke Lovecraft's descriptions rather precisely and seem to have supplanted more than their fair share of the beveled houses and the other enigmatic dwellings that today's real-estate speculation is taking care to destroy one step at a time. As if it were important to ensure a permanent supply of pied-à-terres for phantoms and extraterrestrials in this arrondissement of Paris. That these fabrications are pure fantasy renders the persistence of such diverse but nonetheless abnormal architecture still more incomprehensible.

Are the tapered hulls of the residences the result of a contradiction between an extant land registry and the rigorously quadrangular plan drawn up by contemporary urbanists indifferent to vested rights? Do the complex shanties on top of the most recently constructed buildings spring from an architect's caprice or from the hasty proposal of a contractor enamored of science fiction? For my part, I care very little. I am instead preoccupied by the survival, in this neighborhood, of disconcerting habitations that invite daydreams of the sort that ensure the success of fantastical stories. One difference, however: the transformation of a capital city is subject to more vicissitudes and requirements than a few pages dashed off at a chance inspiration. As always, my ambition is to try and discover a common point between the two distant, somewhat incompatible processes.

Now more than thirty years ago, when I began to write, among so many possible subjects, I set myself the task of describing Paris as a semi-fabulous theater where a certain dramaturgy, if not a characteristic mythology had here found its promised land. I endeavored therefore to explain the means and manner of the sudden metamorphosis in the urban setting. At the time, I had only considered purely novelistic experiences, that is to say, those presented as realistic or plausible. I wasn't bold enough to suggest that my methods might also apply to episodes of another kind, involving, for example, the appearance of ghosts, or even extraterrestrials, the possibility of whose existence had been dismissed. Yet the density of a metropolis obviously supplies them with a more mysterious, more labyrinthine milieu, one richer in contrasts than ruined castles and gloomy inns. I required more time to become aware of it.

The evolution of the genre didn't fail to follow the same stages that marked the substitution of the terror of the Fantastic for the marvels of traditional fairy tales, for the gradual preference for the universe of the metropolis over remote landscapes, and for phenomena inadmissible to science over the miracle accepted in advance. In both cases, one had to pass through an intermediate stage: the supernatural explained. Nevertheless, for Paris, things went very slowly. The well-lit neighborhoods and public monuments never seem to have been besieged by actual phantoms. I wonder how they got so lucky.

The repeated death of the elected members of the Académie Française at the moment they begin the solemn reading of their acceptance speeches isn't attributable in the final analysis to a truly haunted Chair, nor the horrors of the Opéra cellar and the toppling of its chandelier to an implacable specter. The criminal shade Belphegor who appears and disappears in the Salle des Dieux Barbares in the Louvre isn't the reincarnation of a Phoenician God. Every time, the supernatural nightmare is cleared up like a whodunit, just as the fake specters of the mystery novel reveal themselves at the end to be ruffians in disguise. And Fantômas is a phantom in name only.[6]

Paris remains confined in medieval superstition, more impish than anguished. The tradition of the

Enchanted Hand didn't die with Gérard de Nerval. Specialists sometimes prolonged it, not without cleverness. On the contrary, the genuine Fantastic, necessarily concealed, doesn't easily acclimate to Paris. Yet it alone could introduce the scandal of a terrifying supernaturalism into the banal hustle-bustle of daily life, into tax offices, subway trains, into the interiors of public buildings, or behind the dark or well-lit windows of apartment blocks.

Even Fargue's story isn't as clear-cut as it seems. Its ambiguous title, *The Drug*, leaves the objective existence of the beings it follows shrouded in mystery. Maybe they are only hallucinated fantasies in the mind of the author, sprawled out on his mat, opium pipe in hand. Jacques Yonnet's story collection, which forms perhaps the most ingenious attempt to introduce the hereafter into urban life, relies on sorcery and the diffuse magic of quacks and necromancers instead of on the evil-doing of specters whose existence reason cannot accept. The writer, at any rate, didn't persist along this path and died without leaving successors.[7]

In fact, everything happens as if the great overpopulated centers characteristic of contemporary industrial, bureaucratic civilization, already glutted, were loathe to produce the specific imaginary population that humans have always liked to pretend accompany them from a distance and intervene unexpectedly in their daily lives. The ancient world had, on the one hand, its nymphs and its hamadryads, and on the other, its striges and harpies; the forest had its sorcerers and its ogres; the mines, their helpful or mocking dwarfs. Only yesterday, tombs were supposed to contain vampires and rundown houses, ghosts. I admire that until now, the city—perhaps rightly, since it packs a multitude of existences into a limited space—hasn't given birth to beings whose role requires what I would call *a slightly vertiginous open-mindedness*, comparable to the role always assumed in earlier societies by creatures sufficiently adapted to the purpose. These were creatures whose only assigned task, in the final analysis, was to be supernatural, to be, in a sense, our auxiliaries, and not to beggar our disbelief. But then, skepticism has always been a weakness of mine.

Of course, by definition, there is nothing in the metropolis that can't be pinpointed exactly. The crowd of passersby, the interdependence of everyone on everyone else, the network of public services, from the police to garbage collectors, postal workers, bus drivers, each of whose administrative duties excludes the existence of all unknown, isolated space (a desert or a swamp, for example) whose natural defenses are forbidding enough to make it lengthy, difficult, or dangerous to venture there. Yet the same safe havens are necessary in order to conceive of "different" creatures—guardian angels or evil demons, but beings that are essentially "other"—the presence of which the human species, for whatever reason, seems to have a persistent need, and, as I have already noted, *without having to genuinely believe in them*. They are a quasi-ludic unit of an ideal insurance policy perhaps intended to better safeguard the game itself, that is to say, freedom of mind.

I'm now sure it was these beings manqués I was dreaming of when I realized that for a long time I'd already had it in my head to catalogue the beveled houses and absorbent dwellings of the fifteenth arrondissement. They would bring my future interlopers the necessary haunts, the incredible safe havens—the impregnability they lacked. I am now driven to determine the nature of the hosts, identified at last. If there really exists a logic of the imaginary, it should now be possible for me to indicate its probable if not inevitable characteristics, much as a chemist would do for a periodic table that did not yet contain a single element.

I felt an undeniable pull before the disconcerting habitations. On the other hand, contemporary idioms lack the very shades I vaguely supposed to be required by my—truth be told—reckless conception of mythology. Without fail the flat houses would accommodate tenants fabulous and fluid, identical in appearance to human beings, who were nonetheless capable, when the time came, of shrinking little by little to the thickness of a piece of paper in order to make themselves comfortable in the beveled buildings. That this one or that one was demolished wouldn't matter, if one worked to replace them progressively by others, like those of the Villa Croix-Nivert, which offered comparable benefits.

Thus it was a question, in the first place, of ductile creatures capable of mimicry, able to trick humans, borrowing our customs and our appearance, but without feeling our emotions, or sharing our philosophy, never quite comfortable in our atmosphere, let alone in our company, entering into it or vanishing from it only by the *feeder points* and *escape hatches* intuited by Fargue. These are counterfeit beings, to be sure, yet they are not the resurrected or old-fashioned specters at odds with the hereafter. They are distant voyagers, radically *incompatible* with our species, incompatible, as it were, autonomastically. They come from another planet, a parallel universe, possibly non-physical; they might well have been built, in my opinion, from a mixture of tissues uniting the most useful properties of inert matter and, if I may speculate further, a heightened sensibility.

Essentially inhuman, on earth they are nothing but drifters—that is to say, without citizenship or fixed residence. Not that they can't live in an apartment made available to them by casual acquaintances or obtain stolen or falsified identity cards, but in so doing they would only end up exposing the existence of a network which would ultimately lead to their further isolation. Or they could fabricate identity documents themselves, but these still wouldn't correspond to anything certified or verifiable. They find themselves forced to stay in dense urban areas. For if it is possible to prevent *nomads* from entering villages, where monitoring is easy and where everyone knows each other, the same measure would be pointless in a metropolis, where anyone, even a wanted criminal, can pass unobserved, if not flourish. Captive of the city, the extraterrestrial can't rely on any help, nor can he work his way into the system. He will never be a true "resident." He receives no mail, pays no taxes, isn't registered with a single institution, has no documents, whether a birth certificate or a rent receipt. He thus reveals—and for the moment, in this respect alone—his difference from human beings. This is the first red flag, just as in the past a demon could be identified by his cleft hoof or a vampire by his prominent incisors and pointed ears.

The phantom intruder in the metropolis, whose essential nature I am venturing to deduce, necessarily fulfills the condition of being *legally nonexistent*. He doesn't differ physically. He fools the best observer. He is betrayed, not by visible stigmata, but by his administrative nothingness, which, let's admit, is perfectly compatible with one of the most important characteristics of modern civilization. Only later is another kind of index, borrowed from the toolkit of the sciences, called upon. He reacts to this or that stimulus devised by a suspicious expert. The visitor is non-combustible or corrosive, transparent under black light or sensitive to ultrasonic waves: there even exist people like me who perceive them to some extent. One need only carry out a number of such tests to refine and update the properties of old-style phantoms that cast no shadow or have no reflections in mirrors.

I'm not entirely convinced of the accuracy of my line of reasoning. Forged documents, as everybody knows, are a common solution for those without an acceptable legal status. I wonder if it isn't instead the feeling of being forever an *outsider*— an obsession that eventually becomes intolerable— which ultimately puts the safety of the foreign being at risk. To the creature that is incomplete or different, if I may so extend my argument, his partial identification with humans suggests that he actually is one, except of course for certain deficiencies or powers or some unpleasant moments of doubt or melancholy that everyone, moreover, can also experience. Abruptly introduced to life on earth, he is born at whatever age, his mind thoroughly populated with imaginary but coherent memories. The alien weaves himself into into the very fabric of contemporary life, which he participates in from the moment of his arrival on the planet just as totally as anyone who is a rightful citizen of the world. However, several objections come to mind. In the first place, the *non grata* must get a human body and human clothes from somewhere. Next, memories are almost always shared and are concerned with events and episodes that leave a trace. They can't be created from scratch, arbitrarily. Finally, our newcomer must not suffer from haziness or memory lapses starting from a particular day, as if he had retrograde amnesia. Therefore it's best to assume he takes advantage of the death of a loner, infiltrating his corpse in the nick of time. He thereby usurps an appearance, a personality, and memories. As such opportunities are rare and most often unpredictable, I have to believe the impostor must, every once in a while at least, cause them or precipitate them. In a word, his earthly existence begins with a kind of murder, committed, it is true, against someone who is not yet his fellow man, but who becomes so by the very act. No matter. The murderer forgets his crime at the very moment he absolutely and totally assumes the identity of his victim. Those close to the evicted notice nothing, especially after a short adaptation period when they may find themselves surprised by some unexpected reactions. But it's nothing that isn't quickly sorted out. Nevertheless, as a precaution, it is no doubt preferable that the break-in takes place far from the friends and family of the individual. (I reason so well that my lucidity seems to me almost prophetic. At any rate, it's not the first time I've noticed how well vanity and deductive vertigo complement each other.)

Even if the usurper has found a hideout, he still isn't unassailable, because he remains of a different nature than that of real humans. He's — how shall I put it? — neither native-born nor genuinely physical. I imagine him in a situation analogous to that of the conspirators of the Club of Eleven, invented by André Salmon, who were so secretive that they did not even know they were members of the same group. For all their discretion, they didn't run any less risk of being exposed.[8]

Similarly the interloper's condition resembles that of a persistent dreamer who inevitably imagines being woken up, who would not know how to wake himself up, but whom someone else could easily awaken. From this perspective we're all in the same boat: you could unwittingly be one of those fake men and, as for myself, I could be one too.

See what follies drive the daydreams I serve up as reasoning by sprinkling my conjectures with hints of logic. I'd better return to more objective considerations, ones based on an observation of the evolution of the fable from its earliest origins.

Despite their fundamental differences, there is a common trait among the protagonists of marvelous stories, fairy tales, and science fiction. If you ignore the puerile or commercial aspects of each of these genres, in which the author cynically banks on overstated contrasts, you will notice that a supernatural being, God or genie, ghost or extraterrestrial, almost inevitably has a nature radically foreign to that of the human species. At the same time, he takes on human form as he pleases and in perfect fashion, finally revealing himself at a time of his choosing, or conversely, is forced to reveal himself by an ingenious or intrepid hero. The story generally comes to an end at the moment in which its true identity, in one way or another, is revealed.

Today, in the industrial and bureaucratic city, the heterogeneous being, while still endowed with the same quality of being serenely triple and unique, no longer comes from an alternate and hermetically sealed universe like the kingdom of the fairies or the kingdom of the dead. He continues to need a line of credit from the worldview of the age. He borrows its most widespread beliefs, whether they are true or not. One imagines him hurled from the far end of stellar space or germinating from some cosmic chance or error out of the vast pool of possible essences. Benevolent or malevolent, but always also impenetrable and frozen. No doubt indiscernible in its first stage, it is *dual*, equally fascinating and complimentary. He must cause the same irrational panic as his old-fashioned predecessors. Reflecting developments in the sciences, nature has granted him what he requires to meet the demands of the urban hive. At the same time, he is unacceptable to the hive; it is allergic to him. Because he represents the being that tolerates neither constraints or artifices and will lead an existence in outer space that is perhaps more fraternal, powerful, and free; that is, from the hive's perspective, a nonexistence. Instead of imagining or even deducing this species, I was almost seized by the desire to belong to it.

The chimerical being would never have emerged if he didn't correspond to the longings and aspirations of society. He is its fabulous, invulnerable projection; sometimes its mirror image.

I am pleased that my repeated, attentive strolls had finally lead me to the audacious enterprise of deducing, in a quasi-syllogistic manner, the characteristics of future phantoms. Unfortunately I have amused myself for too long, spotting decoys and purposeless traps. They stimulated an idle imagination that I granted leave to drift at will. Now it tires me. The point of my long rambles escapes me. My cogitations now strike me as specious, paralyzing my very ability to think. I give up. I am panic-stricken. I've done enough. I have lost the right to continue to write this little guide or to the reflections I've come away with in the process. I feel instead the desire to be guided myself and returned to my home base. I hardly remember having once asked to get mixed up with this world. I pass on foot the high stone ship's bows that were the points of departure for my daydream. I take one last look at the mural that conjured up for me the wall paintings of yesteryear, when advertisement fostered the seeds of fable. I leave the lopsided hovels in a mess atop the severe buildings. I don't even make a detour to avoid the false facades. I see in a new light the solemnity of the École Militaire. It seems more symmetrical than usual. I know well that it isn't and that man is lost in a universe so labyrinthine that not only his reason, but also his imagination is constantly thrown off course.

As dusk falls, I let my steps lead me quite naturally toward the Villa Letellier and its false facade. It's drizzling. It's getting cold. At the end of the blind alley, some gleaner finishes loosening the gigantic key that once served as the sign of a locksmith's shop. I hadn't noticed it before. Undoubtedly, such things are now sought after by collectors. This one seems heavy. And yet it must be hollow. He holds it before him in both hands. He only has a raincoat over his shoulders, which hangs straight down, undisturbed by wind. He's not wearing a mask. I am surprised to see the part of his face between the lower forehead and the upper lip. He isn't hostile, but rather caught off guard, as if I were the strange-looking one. All of a sudden, he stares at me. I guess that he has understood, that he knows. Instantly, I know too. I played at tracking down phantoms: I was the phantom. I identified safe havens for them that could be of use to me, I set the trap where I intended to lure them, and it was there that I suddenly found myself ensnared. To the neighborhood scrap metal merchant, I lost the role of sweet-talker I had hoped to play. I try in vain to convince myself that fatigue or my poor eyesight has made me the victim of an illusion. I am already driven back against the wall with the false facade. It dilutes itself to accommodate me and I feel myself dissolving into it.

At the last second, in a flash of illumination, I see again, for the first time, the distraught face of a young French student, whose conscious life, around 1930, on a clear night in the woods between Jößnitz and Plauen—you could see pine needles glittering on the forest floor—I had gently brought to a close in order to take possession of his body, his identity, and his memories. He was alone. He was coming back from the cinema. He was new to the area.*

*I've forgotten his name. Yet it's the very same one under which I signed all the books I have published for over thirty years.

History of a Metamorphosis

A Little Guide to the Fifteenth Arrondissement for the Use of Phantoms: the somewhat perplexing title of a heterogeneous text. It was written in installments, and it showed. It was composed of three unequal parts. I slipped from one to the other according to the vagaries of memory and thought. The text began with a scrupulous description of the beveled buildings and of the many other architectural oddities that can be found in the neighborhood of Grenelle, followed by an account of the painted advertisements that once hung on the walls and which had struck my youthful imagination. I concluded with an essay of sorts, whose argument was a reprise of two previous studies I had devoted to the evolution of the Fantastic genre from fairy tales to science fiction.[9] In that segment, I attempted to deduce the kind of phantom that would logically correspond to the administrative, bureaucratic, and technological civilization of the metropolis.

One would hardly think a disparate narrative that moves from the realistic to the hermetic to the discursive would make a solid basis for a film, let alone a television show, which blatantly aims to reach a mass audience. However, as luck should have it, the board of the National Audiovisual Institute was chaired by a poet named Pierre Emmanuel, who didn't rule out experimental undertakings. When a producer, Pascale Breugnot, and a director, Pierre Desfons, both known for their dependability and their competence (not to mention their taste for difficulty) proposed to adapt my text to the small screen, he accepted the challenge. They wouldn't let anything stand in their way. With dogged ingenuity, they thought and rethought pages that, for several reasons, must have seemed like provocations. They made it a point of honor (and how could I complain?) to respect a text that was meant to be read rather than listened to and was thus unduly long and, at the same time, overly concise. In any case, they weren't given a single guiding thread, even a vague one, with which to structure something that bore so little resemblance to a story.

To remedy this unfortunate omission, they introduced two characters that would be indispensable to even the ricketiest plot reduced to its most basic expression: my childhood self and the troublesome phantom whom I was following in order to deduce its features. They figured out—by what foresight?—that, without realizing it, I had identified myself with Villiod, the Man with the Key, whose image, staring down at me from the walls of Paris and the white tiles of the stations of the Métro, had made such a great impression on me. They increased his importance in their script and cast me to play him, in addition to the part of the narrator that is normally given to the author.

Of the filming itself, I would have too much or not enough to say. I willingly went along with their recommendations; I felt that my work, in this new form, had become theirs. Nonetheless, I suffered to see it get left behind. To palliate the text's original sin, they had beautifully furnished it with brisk, relevant episodes: a Punch and Judy show, a taxi chase, the phantom sitting down to dinner with a family of humble origins, my childhood self leading the Man with the Key, whom I simultaneously feared and aspired to become, through the corridors of the Métro. In a word, a great many successful interpretations, faithful to the spirit of the text, but which only made me regret not having better appointed it myself. The way it shifted between confession and demonstration became intolerable to me.

I felt ill at ease. I had the impression of being more phantasmagorical than the phantom I was supposed to track down and unmask. It wasn't that my part began with a scene in which a makeup artist touched up my face for a shot and ended with the inverse scene, during which the same hands wiped my face clean of pigments and powder, as if to restore me to reality after a fabulous parenthesis. Since the sequences aren't shot in the order in which they are viewed, and since I didn't appear in every shot, I remained completely unaware of these external signs of my metamorphosis. My sense of unreality instead came from my awareness that I would appear onscreen, to say nothing of the rushes, with Villiod's cape, mask, and key: this is how I was reunited with a character who, stepping out of a poster, had barely spoken a word to anyone in years. When they saw me in costume, the children in the street spontaneously recognized me, despite the gigantic key, as a hero from a more familiar universe: the legendary Zorro. I was fictional twice over.

At the same time, the incorrigible synthesizing tendency of my mind was causing me to worry. I was anxious to discover the means to ensure the coherence of an almost hour-long performance that couldn't very well consist in a simple representation of the drift of an imagination—still less of an imagination as cerebral as mine.

By the time filming had wrapped, I was still nowhere near the solution. Then, all of a sudden, it came to me: in order to discover how everything fit together, it sufficed that during the course of the action, the narrator (that is, me) would be finally forced to recognize himself as a phantom—or that contemporary stand-in for phantoms, the extraterrestrial—that is, a supernumerary who has surreptitiously wormed his way into the milieu of the metropolis. As a precaution, the intruder, with whom from then on I was to be identified, is never conscious of his alien origins: either he is never informed of them or he has forgotten them at the moment of interchange. But certain traces of his former condition remain in him (in me), and an inexplicable foreboding would come to trouble him. Hence his need for laws of a mathematical rigorousness. The alien hasn't only seized a body that had been made available to him—it hardly matters how—but perhaps more importantly a consciousness whose every memory became his own; and not only memories, but also tastes, ambitions, idiosyncrasies, caprices, still unarticulated hopes, and future weaknesses. In short, the innumerable remainders that defy expression and remembrance, whose totality comprises the *inimitable savor* that each person finds only in himself; as if each heart, injected with the venom of the serpent sketched by Paul Valéry, were made to fall in love with its own singularity.

From that point on, each of the alterations I had to make was given to me in advance. All were derived from the same principle and each had inevitable consequences. The denouement, which had until then escaped me, now imposed itself without the least bit of ambiguity. All that was left for me to do was to clear the ground for it by establishing landmarks along the way. At first, these were to be barely perceptible, with a significance the reader would notice only in retrospect; then, cryptic; and finally, dramatically revealed to an attentive mind.

I was surprised how few additions were needed to transform a barely homogenous mixture into a progressive, calculated discovery, in which each element found its proper place as if it had been planted there beforehand. The beveled architecture and my interest in it, my childhood memories and my speculations about phantoms: little by little these would alert the narrator to his own identity and betray his true nature to him.

My guess is that playwrights or, to take another example, the authors of detective novels find themselves faced with such constraints as a matter of course. But they know this up front and so they consider it from the outset, acting in accordance with the rules they have laid down for themselves. I, on the other hand, had allowed my reflections to wander as far as they liked and to find, in their own momentum, the rhythm that would sustain them. Like a novelist, an essayist, or a poet, I didn't deny myself a certain artistic license, which goes along with lyricism instead of treating it like an obstacle.

The extraordinary thing in the case of the *Little Guide* is that none of the episodes the filmmakers used to introduce the characters captured my attention, nor did I integrate them into the modified version of my text. However, I remain convinced that without the changes they introduced, without the chance necessity of adapting the text into a television show and thus of giving it a plot that was to some extent consistent with a discourse intended to be read (and read attentively, moreover), the idea never would have come to me to link up the three loosely composed parts whose underlying unity they had been the first to bring to light. Much less would I have believed that the transition from an almost total absence of organic unity to an at times punctilious rigor could be effected at so little cost.

Sometimes it seemed to me that the original text was only waiting for such a fortuitous interference to crystalize, since I neither sought it out nor exposed myself to it. Not that I explicitly objected either; on the contrary, I waited with patience and pleasure to learn what would come out of it.

Nor was I able to guess when the transformation of these pages would become definitive. But because of it, the pages attained autonomy, or else the persuasive impact they previously lacked, which had kept them from *sowing hyperbolic doubt concerning the continuity or the identity of the self* in the mind of the reader. Through the description of abnormal buildings, incomplete reminiscences, and a subjective if not specious line of reasoning, I had indirectly tried to infect the reader with precisely this intuition. But the decisive argument was still missing. What I mean is the irrefutable sophism, the quibble that bewitches the intelligence, and to which real life offers no antidote—a little like the arrow and the tortoise used by the Eleatics to refute motion, or the image of the butterfly summoned up by the Taoists to cast doubt on the difference between dreaming and waking, or, with regard to the omnipotence of God, the question of whether he can create a stone so heavy even he cannot lift it.

These are theoretical questions that cause difficulty as a result of the way they are posed. No one ever finds themselves in a situation where they are forced to take them seriously. Nevertheless, they invite the mind to keep the real at arm's length, a detachment from which it comes to draw a serenity that is neither without grandeur, nor certain advantages. The Sword of Damocles that is for each of us the inevitability of death, no doubt needlessly terrifies us. But it might also lead us to a wisdom that could not otherwise be attained.

I'm quite partial to the collection of such logical dead ends. Nothing would satisfy me more than to have contributed in some small way to making the list of them a little longer. One of them, in a way, appears fictionalized in the definitive version of the *Little Guide*. Perhaps I will have the occasion to formulate it rigorously. It was incubating, I believe, in some of my previous stories.

The opportunity presented by the television program put me on the trail. Undoubtedly, I can't rule out the hypothesis—which would contradict me on an essential point—that a nature as deadly or relatively despotic as the one I ascribe to the hidden syntax of the imagination, and which presides over the legitimate connections of reverie as it slides down its steepest slope, could very well have, without this unexpected encounter, suggested some equivalent, or at least parallel solution. The fact remains that I had neglected descriptions and reflections: indeed, it was during the mandatory downtime between the monotonous retakes that another, more convincing arrangement of the scattered data ripened in my idle yet charged imagination.

These days I am not the only one—not by a long shot—to inquire into the workings of the imagination, how it is surprised to catch itself following some particularly ill-defined plan it often only identifies midway through its journey. Among many others that might be more persuasive, I put forward, as evidence of this phenomenon, a comparison of the two versions of the *Little Guide*. I would like to add that, in this case, I am far from displeased that circumstances—which are by nature contingent—were able to provide me with the very insights a protracted mental struggle could not. This seemed to me both the confirmation and the other side of a way of thinking that, despite the contrast between them, triangulates just as surely as it wanders.

In my works I have tackled many different subjects. Perhaps they aren't as unlike as they seem.

An arrangement may one day come into focus, as from the scattered pieces of a puzzle. It would be enough if the same grace that came to the aid of the *Little Guide*, would favor, on a different scale, this time by a most improbable chance, the collection of my earlier research. Then again, hope springs eternal. Today, almost assiduously, I pray that time will finally grant me—and it little matters by what unforeseen detour—a glimpse of the overall picture, where each of my works will find its place.

Author's Note

All the buildings that are referred to in the *Little Guide*, including the false house on the Villa Letellier, are real and their description is rigorously precise. If the curious reader doesn't find them at the addresses indicated, it's because new buildings have replaced them. The neighborhood is in a state of continual reconstruction.

Translator's Notes

P. 7
1. Caillois coined the term "Fantastic" to refer to a genre of fiction that treated the supernatural as if it could be explained in the language of the sciences. Léon-Paul Fargue (1876–1947) was a poet and essayist associated with the symbolist movement in France.

P. 13
2. Here the author has confused Robert Daumier, the realist painter, with Honoré Daumier (1808–1879), the caricaturist.

P. 17
3. Here the author presumably means Leonetto Cappiello (1875–1942), the Italian-born painter and caricaturist whose posters for a wide variety of consumer products in fin-de-siècle Paris earned him the title "the father of modern advertising."

P. 17
4. Hélène de Vogüé (1908–2003). French socialite nicknamed "Nelly" by her lover Antoine de Saint-Exupéry.

P. 30
5. Three towns that appear in the "weird fiction" stories of H. P. Lovecraft (1890–1937), sometimes thought to be fictionalized versions of locations in Essex County, Massachusetts.

P. 32
6. The above paragraph alludes to the plots of *The Haunted Chair* and *The Phantom of the Opera* by Gaston Leroux (1868–1927), *Belphegor* by Arthur Bernède (1871–1937), and the *Fantomâs* series by Marcel Allain (1885–1969) and Pierre Souvestre (1874–1914) respectively.

P. 33
7. Jacques Yonnet (1915–1974). Writer and artist best known for his book *Rue des Maléfices*.

P. 40
8. André Salmon (1881–1969). Poet and art critic best known for his popularization of cubism. His story "Archives of the Club of the Eleven" was

privately circulated among a coterie that included Picasso, Max Jacob, and Guillaume Apollinaire.

P. 47
9. In 1966, Caillois published two volumes of *Anthology of the Fantastic*, a collection of Fantastic and proto-Fantastic stories from around the world, including many of the ones that are mentioned in the *Little Guide*. His other writings on the subject include *At the Heart of the Fantastic* (1965) and "The Natural Fantastic" (1970).

Roger Caillois

Born in Rheims in 1913, Roger Caillois was a literary critic, philosopher of science, novelist, and sociologist best known for his studies of religion, myth and games. Initially associated with the surrealists, he fell out with André Breton after a disagreement about the nature of the Mexican jumping bean, and went on to found the Collège de Sociologie with fellow excommunicants Michel Leiris and Georges Bataille. From this fruitful collaboration emerged *Myth and Man* (1938) and *Man and the Sacred* (1939), his groundbreaking investigation into the relationship between the sacred and transgression. An outspoken agitator against fascism, Caillois spent the war years in Buenos Aires, where he met the leading lights of the Latin American avant-garde. Following his return to France, he joined UNESCO and used his position as the head of the translation program there to introduce the work of Jorge Luis Borges, Pablo Neruda, and Octavio Paz to the French reading public. He was elected to the Académie Française in 1971. In 1978, the year of his death, Caillois published his autobiography *The River Alpheus*, for which he was awarded the Prix Marcel Proust and the Prix Européean de l'Essai Charles Veillon.

Readux Books
Series n°5

*Excellent little books
available at www.readux.net and
in all of the best bookstores*

1. Suburban Wonder *Francis Tabouret*
2. City Spaces *Annett Gröschner*
3. The Idea of a River *Paul Scraton*

As he strolls the streets of Paris's fifteenth arrondissement, Roger Caillois imagines the phantoms that inhabit the modern metropolis, drawing on everything from science fiction and the detective novel to urban mythology. A playful piece of surrealist *flaneurie* and psychogeography, *A Little Guide* is a treasury of Caillois's diverse interests and an homage to the slice of Paris where he spent the better part of his life.

"Caillois...emphatically investigates hidden meanings and scans the deepest horizons of time into infinity: the world turns into an inexhaustible book written in hieroglyphics."
Maria Warner

ISBN 978-3-944801-33-9